# LOG CABIN COOKING

*by*

# Barbara Swell

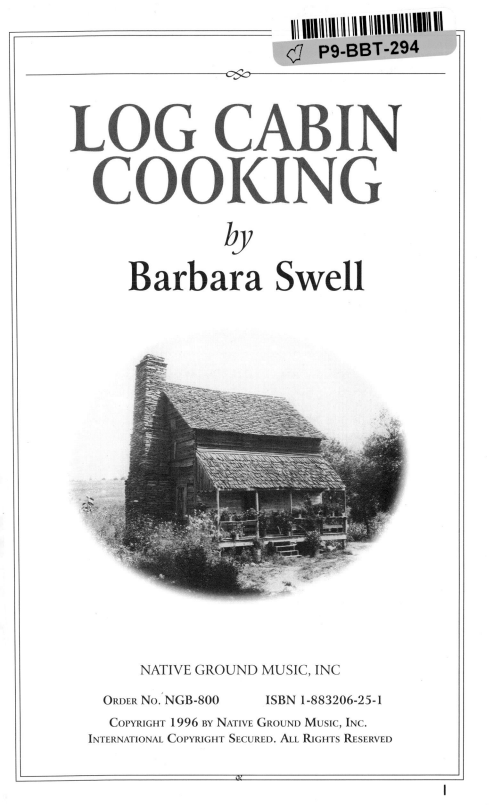

NATIVE GROUND MUSIC, INC

Order No. NGB-800          ISBN 1-883206-25-1

# ONCE UPON A TIME...

Imagine yourself packing up your cherished belongings, leaving behind all but the most essential items needed for survival. It's 1835, you're saying goodbye to friends and relations...maybe forever. You and your family are loading the wagon for an adventure into parts unknown; hoping to outrun the Cholera, food shortages, and have some land to call your own. Maybe you'll land in the mountains, perhaps the prairie. One thing's for certain, your survival will depend on hard work and resourcefulness. And life might be better.

As you settle in after your long journey, most of your time and energy goes into food gathering and storage for the coming winter. Good thing for all those work bees you'll be attending with your new neighbors. Bean stringin's, corn shuckin's, cider makin's, hog slaughterings, and apple parin's. What's going to keep you alive now is independence and self-sufficiency tempered with a strong sense of community. That and maybe some tasty food to warm your innards! You have two iron pots to cook with and the only receipts (recipes) you have are the food rhymes you heard your mama sing as she cooked. Never mind, you have a keen eye, a good sense of smell, and you've been cooking since you were old enough to throw rocks at chickens!

A century and a half has come and gone. We hunt for food at the supermarket, and we're busy with work and play instead of food growing and preserving. But if there's even a little bit of pioneer spirit still in you, take leave of your cookbooks and kitchen gadgets and try your hand at some make-do pioneer cooking. The recipes in this book make use of ingredients that would have been available on the American frontier 150 years ago, but you can throw in anything you think would taste good.

-ENJOY!!!

# CONTENTS

*Anybody can cook. You just have to know what good food tastes like!*
-Maude Smith

# MAKE-DO COOKING

Pioneer cooking was at best "make do" with what you have on hand. Few cooks had measuring instruments, so they became good at "eye-balling" amounts of ingredients needed and textures and quantities of foods they were preparing. **The recipes in this book are intentionally vague.** That's the fun of old-timey cooking. ALL great cooks are resourceful. Give it a go!

## GENERAL RULES FOR MAKE-DO COOKING:

1. **No whining**, i.e. "I can't make that recipe...I don't have turbinado sugar." Figure out a substitute!

2. **Be a risk taker and a good sport.** If you guess at how much of something to use, or experiment with different combinations of ingredients, the chances are in your favor for creating better food. However, **do not take risks** with fresh berries, especially if you spent hours picking them! Practice with something like apples.

3. **Cook by feel.** Notice how a teaspoon of salt looks and feels in your hand. Feel the weight of a cup of sugar. Notice the texture of a medium batter. What does soft butter the size of an egg look like? Taste your food as you go along, adjust seasoning when needed.

4. **Don't time your food with a timer.** Get used to peeking. Cakes are one of the only foods that don't like to be peeked at, especially in the beginning. If you need a timer because you're afraid you'll forget, then you're doing too much. Slow down, hang around the kitchen and pay attention to how your food smells when it's finished cooking.

5. **Be a junior chemist.** Here are some basic rules that the resourceful cook keeps in mind:
- One teaspoon baking powder raises one cup flour.
- To make bread, use one cup liquid to three cups flour and one package dried yeast to two cups liquid.
- To make muffins, use one cup liquid to two cups flour.
- One teaspoon soda is used with one pint sour milk, and with one cup molasses.

# FOOD SOURCES

The recipes in this book have been chosen to reflect foods available to early American pioneers in the 1800's. Families were in survival mode, and were thus consumed with hunting, growing, and preserving food. The pioneer housewife was dubbed "the kitchen queen," and so was responsible for most of the cooking. She also tended numerous children, farm animals, and the garden. Then she got to do the cleaning, washing, sewing, quilting, and mending. Little wonder that the food she prepared was simple and hearty. Perhaps your taste in food is also not complex; but in case you're more adventuresome, ideas have been added to "doctor" up recipes (from items probably not available to pioneers).

## PIONEER FOOD SOURCES CONSISTED OF:

- **Domestic animals:** cows, pigs, goats, turkeys, chicken, oxen sheep, geese.
- **Fish.**
- **Wild game:** birds, rabbits, squirrel, opossum, raccoon, deer, elk, bear, buffalo.
- **Vegetables from the garden:** with seeds brought with them on their journey, traded, or bought from the general store.
- **Crops:** corn, corn, and corn. Maybe wheat and rye.
- **Items bought or traded** at the general store or elsewhere.

Photo: Blue Ridge Parkway

### Food Proverbs

- *Kissin' wears out-cookin' don't.*
- *Them that works hard, eats hardy.*
- *A woman can throw out more with a spoon than a man can bring in with a shovel.*

# THE COUNTRY STORE

T he country store was a pioneer lifeline. Folks knew to settle within a few days ride of the nearest one. Unfortunately, you took your life in your own hands when purchasing foodstuff at the store as there were no laws protecting consumers. Storekeepers counted on the honesty of suppliers, and they were often "had." Butter could be bad in the middle and fresh on the outside, pepper was often laced with gypsum, and flour might be mixed with plaster. Still, a few items were worth the risk involved:

## ESSENTIAL ITEMS

- Coffee beans (to be roasted and ground at home)
- Saleratus (baking soda)
- Tartaric acid (cream of tartar)
- Salt (to preserve and for flavor)
- Flour
- Molasses and sugar compressesd in loaves, either brown or white
- Spices (ginger, cinnamon, cloves, vanilla, rose water, pepper, mace)

## LUXURY FOODS

Salt pork, dried fruits and vegetables, a few canned goods (especially toward the end of the century), whiskey, cheese, dried and pickled fish, striped candy sticks and peppermint balls, rice, dried beans, corn meal, tea, brown sugar, seasonal local fruits and vegetables, eggs and butter.

### Food Insults

- *"He doesn't know twice around a broomstick."*
- *"She doesn't know enough to suck alum and drool."*
- *"She doesn't know beans from bird eggs."*
- *"He looked like death eating crackers."*

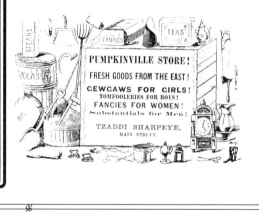

# WHERE TO COOK

## FIREPLACE COOKING

Hearth cooking was the only way for early pioneers to prepare their meals until cookstoves came into popularity in
the late 1800's. The fire provided heat and light, as well
as a place to prepare food. Kettles were hung on poles built into
the fireplace. Other foods were prepared in the coals or on pots
over the coals. The lucky family had an oven for bread baking
built into the hearth. A fire was built in the oven and allowed to
burn down, then the ashes were swept out and the bread was put
in to bake.

## COOKSTOVE COOKING

The early stoves had no temperature guages, so housewives regulated temperatures by size and type of wood. Hardwood makes a
steady hot heat that burns at the same temperature for a long
time. To maintain a constant temperature, medium-sized pieces
of wood were added in steady quantities as the food cooked.

## OVEN TEMPERATURE TESTING:

**Quick** oven (400°-450°): Hand can be held in oven 35 seconds.
**Moderate** oven (350°): Hand can be held in oven 45 seconds.
**Slow** oven (200°-300°): Hand can be held in oven 60 seconds.

Edward M. Ball Collection Asheville,

*"All systematic house-
keepers will hail the day
when some enterprising
Yankee or Buckeye girl
shall invent a stove or
range with a thermom-
eter attached to the oven,
so that the heat may be
regulated accurately and
intelligently."* [1]

(1883)

# COOKING EQUIPMENT

**P**ioneer housewives prior to the late 1800's cooked all their meals in the fireplace with the precious little cast iron and tin cookware they carted in covered wagons over mountains and prairies to their homesteads. Luxuries such as eggbeaters (invented in the 1870's) and pudding molds were seldom found in a pioneer cabin.

## TYPICAL FRONTIER COOKING EQUIPMENT:

- Square trenchers (plates) made of wood
- Spoons, carved of wood
- Teacups and tumblers brought from home
- Cast iron stewpot that hung in the fireplace from a wood or iron lug pole
- Dutch oven, also called a bake kettle for baking breads
- Griddle made from cast-iron or soapstone
- Spider (cast iron skillet on legs with a long handle)
- Tin Bake Oven (a spit for roasting meat with back open to be placed next to the fire.)

## Food Proverbs:

- *The past is a bucket of ashes.*
- *Hope is a good breakfast but a bad supper.*

# Measurements

A rmed with only a teacup, spoon, a keen eye, and a good memory, early American pioneers had to be resourceful when it came to measuring ingredients for cooking. Here's a list of rough equivalents that aided the pioneer cook in "eyeballing" the correct amounts of ingredients needed. In the spirit of frontier resourcefulness, many of the recipes included in this book are "inexact," requiring the cook to become intimate with taste, textures, and appearance of food in various states.

## BUTTER

1 Tbs. (heaped) =size of a hickory nut
2 Tbs. (heaped) = the size of an egg (1 stick)
4 Tbs. ( heaped) = one teacup (2 sticks)
1 lb. butter = 2 teacups well packed (4 sticks)

## FLOUR, MEAL, SUGAR, COFFEE

5 Tbs. sifted flour or meal (heaped) = one teacup
1 Tbs. sugar (heaped) = one oz.
7 Tbs. granulated sugar (heaped) = one teacup
1 lb. granulated sugar  = 2 teacups (level)
1 lb. sugar = 2 1/2 teacups (level)
1 lb. coffee = two teacups (heaped)
1 qt. meal = 3 1/2 teacups (level)
1 lb. sifted flour = 4 teacups (level)

## LIQUID

8 oz. = one teacup
1 gill = 1/2 teacup

"Corn Shuckin,"

# WHEAT

L et's say you were lucky enough to grow wheat or buy flour, how would you get your bread to rise? Commercial yeast and baking powders were not widely available until the later part of the 19th century, providing yet another opportunity for pioneer resourcefulness. Baking soda, called saleratus, was very available and when combined with sour milk produced the carbon dioxide needed to lighten bread. Homemade baking powder was made by combining saleratus with cream of tartar (not as available) and corn starch. Some 19th century cookbooks suggest that baking powder could be created from the ashes of corncobs.

Bread was leavened by homemade yeast made from boiling hops, or by natural fermentation which yielded either sourdough or salt-risin' bread. These natural processes are still used today by great bakers. Sourdough bread from wild yeast takes some time and effort, but is well worth the energy. The process is quite lengthy, and an abbreviated version follows. Novices will need to consult a bread-baking book for more specific instructions. Salt risin' bread is tasty but it will smell you and yours out of your home while you're preparing it!

### 1883 Bread-baking Attire

*"A neat calico apron with bib, and sleeves of dress well-tucked up and fastened so that they will not come down, add much to the comfort of this, the most important task of the kitchen queen."* [1]

## 1848 ADVERTISEMENT: "BE CAREFUL WHAT YOU EAT"

BORWICK'S Baking Powder was the first, and is the best Baking Powder. Its merits are too well known to require any puffing by the proprietor. Warranted free from alum, found in most of the worthless imitations. Try it once, and you will never use the trash recommended by unprincipled shopkeepers. As you value your health, insist upon having Borwick's Baking Powder only.

# WHEAT

## SALT RISIN' BREAD

**Sponge:**

1/2 cup sliced potato
1/2 tsp. salt
1 Tbs. white corn meal

1 Tbs. flour
2 cups boiling water

Let mixture set 15 hrs. Keep warm. Foam should form. Pour water off top and discard potato. Add enough flour to make consistency of cake batter and let rise until double. Mix, then add to sponge:

2 cups flour
1/2 tsp. salt
2 Tbs. sugar

Butter the size of an egg
2 cups warm water

Add in about 2 more cups of flour to make a soft dough and knead 20 minutes. Place in 3 buttered loaf pans and let rise until double. Bake about 40 minutes, starting at 400° for 10 minutes and finishing at 350° for 30 minutes.

## ODORLESS SALT RISIN' BREAD

Pour 1 cup boiling water over 2 medium sliced potatoes. Let stand until lukewarm. Add 1 tsp. salt and 1 tsp. sugar. Stir in flour until you have a heavy batter. Let rise in a warm place until double in bulk. Remove sliced potatoes from dough. Knead, adding flour to keep from sticking, and make into loaves. When doubled, bake 40-45 minutes at 375°.

**\*Note**: This is an old-timey recipe that may or may not actually rise. If you don't mind cheating a bit, add 1 tsp. dried yeast dissolved in 1/4 cup lukewarm water to the batter.

> *In the breadbox of your affections, remember me as a crumb.*

# WHEAT

## WILD YEAST SOURDOUGH BREAD

Allow all day to make this bread. Pioneers made and shared their own starters, and did not add yeast. You needn't add yeast either if you have lots and lots of time and if you have a real good starter.

**Sour Dough Starter:**
4 cups flour
4 cups warm water *(do not use chlorinated water)*
3 Tbs. sugar.
Combine and beat with a wooden spoon until smooth. Place in crockery bowl and cover, let stand in a warm (80°) place about 48 hours until sour and bubbly.

**Sponge:** 1 cup starter, 1 cup warm spring water, 1Tbs. sugar, 2 cups all purpose flour, 1 tsp. yeast. Stir batter until no lumps remain. Let sit for about 4 hours or overnight.

**Bread:** Add to sponge 1 cup warm spring water, 1 tsp. yeast, 3 tsp. salt and enough flour to make a soft dough. Knead 10 minutes or until it's elastic. Let rise until double in bulk at room temperature. Shape into 2 or 3 oblong or round loaves and let rise until double in bulk on a breadboard sprinkled with cornmeal. (Dust top with flour and cover with two kitchen towels). When ready to bake, preheat oven to 375° and place a shallow pan of water on bottom shelf. Slash bread 1/4 in. deep, however you like, to allow for expansion. Bake until brown on a greased cookie sheet, or ideally on a bread stone. If you use a baking stone, put it on the bottom shelf in the oven and your pan of water on the top shelf. Allow bread to cool before you slice, if you can stand it.

**To replenish starter after each use:** Add 1 cup flour, 1 cup spring water, 1 tsp. sugar. Shake well and let it stay at room temp. 6 hours. Then refrigerate and use within 2 weeks.

*To make a good bread, always be up in the morning early, just at the peep of day.[1]*

(1883)

# WHEAT

## BISCUITS

2 cups flour                          3 tsp. baking powder
4 Tbs. shortening (size of an egg)    2/3 cup sweet milk
3/4 tsp. salt

Cut shortening into flour, salt, and baking powder. Add milk, roll out on a floured board and cut into shapes. Bake on a greased sheet in hot (450°) oven until browned.

*Nitty-gritties of good biscuits: Shortening is important-some say solid vegetable shortening works best. Some recipes call for a ratio of 1/2 cup shortening to 2 cups flour, but that's pretty rich for most folks nowadays. Flour is crucial as well. Use a soft winter wheat flour for light biscuits. Don't over-handle your biscuit dough (makes them tough). You can substitute self-rising flour; just omit salt and baking powder.

## BUTTERMILK BISCUITS

Follow the recipe above but substitute buttermilk for the sweet milk, and add 1/3 tsp. baking soda to dry ingredients.

## SCONES

Add to biscuit recipe above, 1 beaten egg to milk, 2 Tbs. sugar, and just a little extra flour to dry ingredients. (Raisins, nuts, dried blueberries, cherries, cranberries, or strawberries adds a nice touch). Divide dough into 2 halves. Roll out each half into a circle onto a board dusted with flour and sprinkled with sugar (thicker than for biscuits). Cut pie-style and bake sugar-side up.

### Biscuit Sayin's
- *He's round as a biscuit.*
- *Take two and butter them while they're hot.*
- *Better the guests wait on the biscuits than the biscuits wait on the guests!*

# WHEAT

## 19TH CENTURY SALLY LUNN

One cup sour milk, one egg, one spoon butter, one teaspoon each of soda and cream of tartar (or 1-2 tsp. baking powder), a little salt, flour enough to make a stiff batter. Bake in a buttered tube pan in a moderate oven until brown and spongy.

N.C. Archives and History

## NICE MUFFINS (1886)

"Two eggs, butter the size of an egg, one cup milk, one Tbs. sugar, one heaping tsp. baking powder, flour to make a stiff batter. Bake in a moderate-hot oven until done."[4]

• *It's a little too much to save,*
*and a little too much to dump.*
*And there's nothing to do but eat it,*
*that makes the housewife plump.*[5]

• *It takes face powder to get your man,*
*But it takes baking powder to keep him!*[5]

# CORN

Morning, noon, and night, the pioneers ate it...boiled, baked, fried, and dried. Corn was the most important crop to the settlers. One acre of corn could produce up to twenty times the yield as an acre of wheat or rye, and it could be planted between tree stumps on uncleared land. Not only did corn provide feed for the family and farm animals, it found it's way into mattresses, pipes, and outhouses. Children made dolls from the shucks, and cooks made baking powder from corncob ashes.

The grist mill needed for grinding dried corn into useable meal was an essential part of the frontier community. You can still buy buhr (stone) ground cornmeal today at historic mills or through the mail (see appendix). Buhr ground cornmeal contains the germ and is best kept frozen. It is very much worth seeking out for baking. Yellow or white? The South swears by white, other regions prefer yellow. Try both!

Photo by Margaret Morley, N.C. Archives and History

## Kitchen Physics:

• *Velocity is what you let go of a hot frying pan handle with.*
• *Half past cornbread and goin on biscuits.*

# CORN

## CORNMEAL MUSH

Boil 2 cups water, add 1/2 tsp. salt, and sprinkle in cornmeal slowly while stirring until mush becomes thick. Eat warm with butter and honey or molasses or put in a bread pan and chill until set. Slice and fry in a frying pan with a bit of butter until crisp on both sides, then serve with maple syrup or honey.

**Polenta:** To warm mush, add parmesan cheese, salt, pepper, garlic, italian herbs to taste, and diced sundried tomatoes. Chill in bread pan, slice, and fry in a small amount of butter or olive oil until brown.

## JOHNNY CAKE IN RHYME

Two cups Indian (cornmeal), one cup wheat;
One cup good eggs that you can eat.
One-half cup molasses too,
One big spoon sugar added thereto;
Salt and soda, each a small spoon.
Mix up quickly and bake it soon.

from: Brenner, *My Folks Come in a Covered Wagon*[9]

## JOHNNY OR JOURNEY CAKE

Make a thick mush, add a pinch of salt, make into small cakes and bake on a greased pan until browned.

### Food Insults
- *He's small potatoes and few to the hill.*
- *He's all vine and no taters!*
- *He flies around like a parched pea in a hot skillet.*
- *He's helpless as spilled beans on a dresser.*

# CORN

## HOE CAKE

Make as Johnny Cake, add a little butter and cook on a clean, greased hoe over hot coals (or you could always use a hot oven).

## HUNTER'S CAKE

Make as Hoe Cake and add a pinch of baking soda. Bake on a board near the fire.

## ASH CAKE

2 cups cornmeal
1 cup buttermilk
3/4 tsp. soda

1/3 cup butter
1 tsp. salt

Clear a spot out of the ashes in the fireplace, drop batter onto the hearth. When the dough forms a crust, cover with ashes and hot coals. Bake until done through about 15-20 minutes.

Edward M. Ball Collection, Asheville, N.C.

*The farm was so steep he could look down the chimney and see what his old woman was fixing for supper.*

# Corn

## Corn Pone

Make a thick mush of 2 cups cornmeal, 1 tsp. salt, and boiling water. Let it cook a few minutes, cool a bit and add 1/2 tsp. soda and 1 beaten egg. Drop onto a hot skillet with butter melted in it and cook in hot oven until brown. Leave a thumb or hand print on top of your pone if you want to be real authentic.

## Cornbread

| | |
|---|---|
| 1 cup cornmeal | 1 tsp. salt |
| 1 cup all purpose flour | 1 cup milk |
| 1 Tbs. sugar | 1/4 cup shortening, melted |
| 3 tsp. baking powder | 1 egg |

Mix dry ingredients together. Melt shortening in oven in a cast iron frying pan. Mix wet ingredients together, then add melted shortening. Combine all, stir briefly and pour into hot greased skillet. Cook at 375-400° for 20-25 min. until browned.

**Tasty additions:** Grated cheese, jalapeno peppers, bacon, corn kernals, sundried tomatoes, chopped roasted peppers.

## Cornsticks

Make as above and pour into a hot, buttered cast iron cornstick pan. Some folks omit the egg.

### To Mend an Iron Kettle:

Mix the white of an egg with some iron filings and some lime to make a thin paste. Apply to the crack and let it set a couple hours.

# CORN

## THOMAS JEFFERSON'S SPOON BREAD

Scald 1 qt. milk and 1/4 tsp. salt. Sprinkle in very slowly 1 cup cornmeal. Cook in a double boiler one hour. Add 3 Tbs. butter and 3 eggs. Mix well. Bake in oven 45 minutes.[15]

## EASIER SPOON BREAD

| | |
|---|---|
| 1 cup cornmeal | 2 cups boiling water |
| 1/2 tsp. salt | 2 eggs, separated |
| 2 Tbs. butter | 1 cup milk |

Add boiling water to cornmeal, salt, and butter and mix well. Cool and add milk and beaten egg yolks. Fold in stiffly beaten egg whites and pour in a greased casserole dish. Bake in a 400° oven for 30 minutes or until brown.

## ROASTED CORN

Corn tastes great roasted. You can take a fresh ear, peel back the husk and remove silk, replace husk, dip in water then grill by fire in the hearth or on the grill outside. Corn can also be roasted on the ear in a frying pan. Just shuck it and roll it around in a hot buttered iron skillet, or try cutting the kernals off and brown them in a bit of butter in a skillet. Add some chopped red bell pepper or some fresh minced herbs (any will do nicely).

# POTAGES (SOUPS AND STEWS)

The authors of the Kansas Home Cook-Book of 1886 remind us that "the modern word for soup is potage and this is used everywhere on bills of fare." Soups and stews were a common meal as the ingredients could be thrown in a large kettle and hung from the fire to simmer all day while the cook tended to her numerous children and countless other chores. Please be sure to heed the "soup warnings" lest your finished product be unwholesome and unsatisfactory!

## 19th Century Soup Warnings

*"Lean, juicy, fresh-killed meat is best for soup; stale meat will make it ill-flavored and fat meat is wasteful."[4]*

*"Soup made of cold meat has always a vapid, disagreeable taste which nothing can disguise."[6]*

*"Every particle of fat should be carefully skimmed from the surface. Greasy soup is disgusting and unwholesome."[6]*

*"Potatoes, if boiled in the soup, are thought by some to render it unwholesome, from the opinion that the water in which potatoes have been cooked is almost a poison."[6]*

## SWEET POTATO-SQUASH SOUP

1 cup milk
4 medium sweet potatoes
2 winter squash (butternut or acorn)

1 can chicken broth
Grated fresh ginger, pepper

Cook potatoes and squash until tender. Scoop out pulp and either mash or puree with a little broth. Add remaining chicken broth, ginger and pepper to taste, and enough milk to suit you and heat, but don't boil. Garnish soup with thin sliced lemon and fresh parsley or cilantro.

# POTAGES

R.H. Scadin Collection, Ramsey Library, UNCA, Asheville.

## PORTABLE SOUP (1845)

"Let beef or chicken soup get cold, skim off every particle of fat. Boil it until thick. Season very highly with pepper, salt, cloves, and mace. Add a little brandy or wine, and pour it over platters not more than a quarter of an inch thick. Let it be till cold, then cut into three inch square pieces. Set them in the sun to dry, turning often. Store them in an air-tight vessel between layers of paper. Whenever you wish to make a soup of them, you have only to put a quart of piping hot water to one of the cakes."[14] (You guessed it....early boullion cubes!!!)
*Caution: These are probably not safe to eat!

> *People who boil and stew soon cook in their own juices.*

# POTAGES

## POTATO SOUP

5 potatoes, peeled and diced
1 onion, chopped
2 carrots, sliced
Chicken or vegetable broth (about 1 1/2 cups)
2 cups milk
Salt and pepper

Saute onion in a little butter. Add broth, potatoes, and carrots. Cook until soft, then mash slightly with potato masher. Add milk, salt, and pepper to taste and heat through but do not boil.

**CORN CHOWDER**: Add fresh, canned, frozen, or creamed corn to broth after potatoes and carrots have cooked. Add milk, and pepper to taste, then heat.

**OYSTER SOUP**: Omit carrot, and add canned oysters and broth after potatoes are cooked. Add milk and pepper to taste and heat.

### Pioneer Etiquette

*When you are at the table, do not eat in a greedy manner, like a pig.*
-McGuffey's 3rd Reader

*Avoid all appearance of haste at the table, but as soon as you are helped, begin to eat. The custom of waiting is obsolete.*[4]

*Fruit is eaten with a silver knife and fork, after which you dip your fingers in the fingerbowl.*
-Kansas Home, 1886

# MEAT AND WILD GAME

Following on the heels of corn, came the second most important food item to pioneers....meat. Domestic farm animals came along with their owners on their journey to unsettled lands. A homestead might have included cows, pigs, goats, turkeys, chickens, oxen, sheep, and geese. With the exception of pigs, few of these animals were eaten as they must provide milk, eggs, and wool. Most meat came from the streams, forests, and the prairie. Wild game included fowl, rabbits, squirrel, opossum, raccoon, deer, elk, and bear. Buffalo were plentiful (numbering in the millions) up until 1890 when they became all but extinct.

Once the hunter killed and dressed his meat, it was then prepared by the cook for immediate eating, or preserved by salting, smoking, or drying. A tin kitchen was the preferred method of roasting meat. This was an open backed tin oven with a spit that was placed with the open side facing the fire in the hearth. Drippings were caught in a tin pan placed under the item to be roasted. Because wild game is lean, cooks usually larded the animal, adding a layer of salt pork under the skin (especially fowl) when roasting. The recipes that follow are examples of how precious meat might have been "stretched" to feed a large family. Prepared, wild game may be substituted for the meat in most of the recipes.

*"R.H. Scadin Collection, UNC-Asheville*

*"Taking the Chicken to Market,*

8

# Meat and Wild Game

## Baked Prairie Chicken (1886)

Stuff the chicken with a prepared dressing of bread, seasoned with butter, pepper, salt, and summer savory. Bind on the outside thin slices of sweet bacon, and baste often while cooking. Remove the bacon before sending to the table.[4]

**Modern version:** Take boneless chicken breasts, wrap each half with a slice of bacon, and bake in the oven until chicken is cooked through.

## Chicken Shortcake

3 cups cooked chicken, cut up
2 Tbs. butter
2 Tbs. flour
1 cup milk
Large pinch dried herbs (options: basil, oregano, thyme)
Salt and pepper to taste

Melt butter in frying pan, add flour and brown. Add milk slowly and stir to keep from lumping. When thickened, add herbs, salt and pepper, and chicken. Serve over cornbread.

## Chicken Pie

Prepare chicken topping as above, and add sauted onions, peas, carrots, cooked potatoes (cubed), and any other vegetables on hand. Spread a thin layer of cornbread on top and bake, or top with a pastry crust and bake in a moderate oven until browned and bubbly.

*Never serve turkey for New Years or you will scratch backwards. Always serve pork so that you can root foreward.*

# MEAT AND WILD GAME

## CHICKEN AND DUMPLINGS

Cook a chicken in salted water. Debone and save broth, skim off all fat.

**Dumplings:**

| | |
|---|---|
| 3 cups flour | 1 1/2 tsp. salt |
| 1 egg | 1 cup milk |

Mix and roll out thin, cut into one inch strips. Allow strips to dry out as you bring broth to a boil. Drop in strips one at a time and cook until tender. Add chicken and 2 cups milk, heat thoroughly, but don't boil. Add salt and pepper to taste.

## BRUNSWICK STEW

This stew was originally made from squirrel meat, but chicken will do as a substitute. The recipe below is from an early 1800's cookbook. To modernize, after chicken is cooked, put ingredients in a crockpot and simmer all day, adding corn a few minutes before you eat the stew. Some like to cook the stew with a few slices of bacon or a piece of salt pork.

Boil a whole chicken until meat is tender and falls off the bone, remove bones. Add to chicken and broth six tomatoes cut up, four ears of corn scraped from the cob, five potatoes, a half-pint butter beans, salt, and pepper. Put it in at an early hour, and let it stew until it becomes thick.

*Courtesy of NC Division of Archives and History*

> • *The fish sees the bait but not the hook.*
> *-Chinese Proverb*
> • *All that is required of in the enjoyment of love or sausages -- is confidence.*
> *-Anonomyous*

# Meat and Wild Game

Among the early American pioneers were immigrants from Germany and Switzerland who settled in Pennsylvania and were known as the Pennsylvania Dutch. Their colorful language was a mixture of English and German. The recipes that follow reflect a combination of German and Swiss influence on pioneer foods.

## Dried Sweet Apple Schnitz
### From Swiss Immigrants in 1860's

Boil either a ham bone or a piece of pork with the desired amount of dried sweet apples and cook until almost tender. Add about one-half as many pared raw potatoes as apples and continue cooking until meat, apples, and potatoes are well done.[7]

## Apples and Buttons (Schnitz un Knepp)

| | |
|---|---|
| 1 pt. dried apples | 1 tsp. salt |
| 1 lb. smoked ham | Pepper to taste |
| 1 Tbs. brown sugar | 1 egg, well beaten |
| 1 cup flour | 3 Tbs. melted butter |
| 2 tsp. baking powder | 1/2 cup milk |

Cover dried apples with water and soak overnight. In the morning, cover ham with water and simmer for 2 hours. Add the apples and soaking water and simmer about 1 more hour. Add the brown sugar.

**Dumplings:** Sift together flour, baking powder, salt, and pepper. Mix together milk, butter, egg and stir into flour quickly until just mixed. Drop by tablespoons into simmering ham and apples. Tightly cover the kettle and cook for 20 more minutes and serve piping hot on a platter.

### Pennsylvania Dutch Sayings
- *Come from the wood-pile in; Mom's on the table and Pop's et himself done, already.*
- *Eat your mouth empty before you say.*
- *The pie is all, but the cake is yet.*

# MEAT AND WILD GAME

Photo by Gideon T. Laney courtesy of David C. Anderson

## SCHNITZ AND KNEPP
*by H. Luther Frees*

I am a man well up in years with simple tastes and few,
But I would like to eat again a dish my boyhood knew.
A rare old dish that Mother made that filled us all with pep,
This generation knows it not-we called it Schnitz and Knepp.
I patronize all restaurants where grub is kept for sale,
But my search up to the present has been without avail.
They say they never heard of it, and I vainly wonder why,
For that glorious concoction was better far than pie.
Dried apple snits, a slab of ham and mammoth balls of dough,
Were the appetizing units that filled us with a glow,
When mother placed the smoking dish upon the dinner table,
And we partook of its delight as long as we were able.
My longing for that boyhood dish, I simply will not shelf;
If I cannot find it anywhere, I'll make the thing myself.[3]

# Meat and Wild Game

## Pigs in a Puddle

1/2 lb. ground meat (beef, turkey, pork)
1 onion, chopped
Binder, can be cooked rice or breadcrumbs
A cabbage
1 qt. tomatoes, stewed or chopped spiced with salt and pepper
Italian herbs to taste

Brown meat and onion and drain off fat. Add cooked rice or bread crumbs. Drop outer leaves of cabbage into boiling water just until softened. Put a spoonful of meat mixture onto each cabbage leaf and roll up egg roll style. Place in a shallow, greased pan. Cover with tomato sauce and bake at 350° about 30-45 minutes until bubbly.

## Cornish Pasties (Meat Pies)

3 potatoes, cut into medium chunks
3 carrots, sliced 1 in. thick
1 onion, chopped
1/2 lb. lean meat (chicken, pork, beef) cut into small chunks
Salt and pepper

Make enough pastry dough for two pies. Roll out into 2 large circles or 5 or 6 small circles if you want individual pies. Combine ingredients and place on front half of circle. Fold crust over ingredients. To seal, put a little water between edges of crust, pinch, then press edges with tines of a fork. Prick crust a few times to allow steam to escape. Bake about 40-50 minutes in a 375° oven or until brown and meat is cooked through.

• *I'm so hungry I could eat a sow and six pigs.*
• *May your friends be many, your troubles few and all your sausages, long.*

# MEAT AND WILD GAME

## SHEPHERD PIE

5 potatoes, cooked and mashed with a little milk, butter, salt
1 lb. ground beef, turkey, or pork
1 onion, chopped
2 tomatoes, peeled and chopped (dip in boiling water to peel)
Salt, pepper, herbs (garlic, oregano, thyme) to taste
3/4 cup water (part of it can be red wine)
1/2 cup grated cheese (optional)

Brown ground meat in frying pan, drain off all fat. Add onion, tomato, water, wine, and spices, and cook until mixture begins to thicken a bit. Put meat mixture in bottom of a casserole dish and carefully spread mashed potatoes on top. Sprinkle with cheese and bake in a hot 450° oven for 15 min.

To make **Cornbread Pie**, add a thin layer of cornbread batter to top of meat ingredients and bake at 400° for 20 minutes until bread is cooked and browned.

•*Nothing helps scenery like ham and eggs.*
        *-Mark Twain*
•*A whistling girl and a crowing hen will always come to some bad end.*

## MEAT HASH

1-3 cups leftover cooked meat finely chopped (chicken, beef, pork)
4 potatoes, diced
1 onion, chopped
Salt and pepper
Butter for frying

Fry potatoes in frying pan until tender. Add onions, meat, and cook until browned. Salt and pepper to taste. Good for breakfast, lunch, or dinner. A pioneer mainstay.

# VEGETABLES

W ith seeds brought from home, traded, or purchased at the general store; pioneers grew corn, wheat, rye, potatoes, turnips, beets, onions, pumpkins, beans, cabbage, carrots, squash, tomatoes, and herbs. While commercially canned foods were becoming popular following the Civil War, the poorest quality of vegetables made their way into the cans, leaving the wise to grow and preserve their own. Vegetables were dried, pickled, or stored in the root cellar for later use. Thomas Jefferson, an enthuiastic gardener, is credited for encouraging Americans to grow and eat tomatoes which had been reputed to be poisonous!

## ZUCCHINI CLARANET

Cut the stalk off of a zucchini plant so that it is hollow on the large end and solid on the small end. To do this, you will slice off the leaf section, being careful not to cut into the hollow part of the stem. Cut a tiny length-wise slit at the small end and place your mouth over the end, covering the small incision...and blow. Be sure to wipe the pricklies off the stem first! The larger the stalk, the deeper the note. Early season stalks work best. Widen the slit if you can't get a sound at first.

Create a band with each musician playing various sizes of squashaphones. Great for summer neighborhood parades!

Rita and Annie Erbsen, Photo by Barbara Swell

# VEGETABLES

## LEATHER BRITCHES

This is an old-timey method of preserving green-beans that was convenient because no canning was needed. Bean stringin' parties made the job more fun. Folks still preserve their beans this way, but the taste is an acquired one. Children love stringing beans, and they look great hanging from the hearth.

Pick your fresh beans, wash and snap stem end off, string if needed. Break in half and run a threaded needle through middle of each bean. When the string is as long as you like, or as much as your string will bear, tie it off and hang in a cool dark place, checking to be sure the beans don't mold, until dry. Some folks unstring dried beans and store in a muslin sack, others leave them strung until time to eat them.

**To Cook:**
Wash beans and soak overnight in cold water. In the morning, strain off water and rinse. Cover with water, add some ham for flavor and simmer for about six hours or until tender.

## BAKED BEANS

2 cups dried navy beans
A few slices bacon (optional)
1 Tbs. brown sugar

1/3 cup molasses
1 tsp. dry mustard
5 Tbs. ketchup

Soak beans overnight, drain and rinse. Cook in fresh water until softened. Pour out liquid and reserve. Fry bacon and add to beans along with other ingredients. Add enough water to cover beans. Bake in a slow 250° oven for at least 3 hours.

## MAUDIE'S CHEESE BISCUITS IN TOMATO SAUCE

One onion, chopped
1 tsp. butter
3 Tbs. flour
1 tsp. sugar
One qt. canned stewed tomatoes or about 7 ripe, chopped, peeled
tomatoes cooked in a pan to release juices.
Dried or fresh herbs (oregano, basil, or thyme)
One cup grated cheddar cheese
One recipe biscuit dough, uncooked

Saute chopped onion in a little butter until translucent. Blend in
flour. Add tomatoes, sugar, salt and pepper. Mix well in a sauce-
pan and bring to a boil. Add herbs, pour into a baking dish, cover
with biscuits, and sprinkle with cheese. Bake in a hot 400° oven
about 15 minutes until biscuits are done and cheese bubbles. Call
everyone to the table and have them ready to eat before you take
the dish out of the oven.

## VEGETABLE CUTLETS

Grate a combination of all the vegetables you have growing in
your garden or that you have on hand (zucchini, yellow squash,
peppers, carrots, corn, green beans, onions).
1 egg
Breadcrumbs enough to bind
Fresh or dried herbs
Salt and pepper to taste

Combine vegetables, egg, and enough breadcrumbs to bind but
keep a bit dry because the crumbs will absorb moisture from the
vegetables. Chill about an hour, then form into patties. Saute in
skillet with a little butter, cooking on low heat until browned and
cooked through. Serve with horseradish sauce or eat as a veggie
burger.

# VEGETABLES

R.H. Scadin Collection, UNCA, Asheville,

*"Plowing in the Mountains"*

## ROOT VEGETABLE PASTIES

1 onion, chopped
3 potatoes, cooked and mashed
3 carrots, sliced
2 turnips, cooked and mashed
A handful of frozen or fresh peas
Herbs, fresh or dried (any will do)
Salt and pepper

You can experiment with any combination of cooked vegetables, anything you include will taste good. Add cheese if you like (grated hard cheese or feta).

Combine ingredients. Make enough pastry crust for two pies. Divide into 8 balls and roll out into circles. Put ingredients onto front of each circle, fold other half over top and seal pastry by pinching together ends (moistened with water) then pressing edges with tines of a fork. Prick a few holes in crust with fork to allow steam to escape. Bake at 400° for 20 minutes or until browned.

*Fine words butter no parsnips.*

# VEGETABLES

## PICKLED RED BEETS

3 lbs. beets                    1/2 cup sugar
2 cups vinegar                  1/2 cup water

Boil beets until tender.  Drain,  remove skins, and slice.  Heat
vinegar, water, and sugar just until boiling.  Add beets and return
to boil then remove from heat.  Pack into sterile jars or store un-
sealed in the refrigerator.  They keep a long time.

## RED PICKLED EGGS

Soak hard boiled eggs in pickled beet juice for about 2 days.
They're attractive and tasty.

## SAURKRAUT (QUICK)

Cabbage, shredded (enough to fill a quart jar)
2 tsp. salt
1 tsp. sugar
1 Tbs. vinegar

Sprinkle 1 tsp. salt in bottom of a glass quart jar; fill jar with
shredded cabbage.  Press down slightly and add 1 tsp. salt, sugar,
and vinegar.  Cover with boiling  water and seal (or let it sit in
refrigerator). It will be ready to eat in about a week.

---

### Stomach Lore

•*A stomach that is seldom empty despises common food.*
*-Horace*
•*It's a strong stomach that has no turning.*
*-Addison Mizner*
•*When the stomach speaks, wisdom is silent.*
*-Arab Proverb*
•*A sharp stomach makes short graces.*
*-Scotch Proverb*

# VEGETABLES

## APPLE AND CARROT SALAD

Grate equal parts apples and carrots. Mix to taste with lemon juice, sugar or honey, and salt. Add chopped nuts or dates, and raisins if you like. You can throw in some crushed pineapple, as well.

## DANDELION SALAD

Young dandelion greens, (picked before plant flowers), rinsed and chilled. Be sure they're herbicide and pesticide free.
Lettuce, washed and torn
Bacon, cooked and crumbled
Egg, boiled and sliced
Grated cheese (Swiss is best)
Edible flowers in season sprinkled on top  (violets, pansies, nasturtiums, calendula)

Toss salad with salt, pepper, and a vinegrette dressing. Try raspberry vinegar, olive oil, salt, and pepper.

Photo by Margaret Morley, NC Archives and History

"At the Tubs"

> *To make a salad dressing, four persons are wanted: A spendthrift, for oil; a miser, for vinegar; a counsellor, for salt, and a madman to stir it up.*
> - *Spanish Proverb*

# FRUIT

W ild and cultivated blackberries, gooseberries, huckleberries, cherries, grapes, and currants graced the tables of the lucky 19th century homesteader. Apples, brought by seed from England were found throughout the West by mid-century largely thanks to the efforts of John Chapman (known to us as Johnny Appleseed). Fruit, mistrusted in the earlier part of the 1800's, was blamed for the Cholera epidemic of 1832. In fact, many settlers fled west to escape Cholera and other then-fatal diseases only to find that they brought the diseases along with them! The authors of the *Kansas Home Cookbook* of 1886 suggested that folks plant the following varieties of fruit in their home garden:

## SUGGESTED FRUIT VARIETIES, 1886

Wilson's Albany and Downer's Prolific Strawberries
Doolittle Raspberries
Kittatinny Blackberry
Houghton Gooseberry
Red Dutch Currant
Early Richmond Cherry
Concord Grape

"Provide all these in plenty, and cultivate well, and the tired, over-worked housewife, gathering her dessert ready cooked, and prepared with a skill no artist can equal, will bless you for your wise forethought, that will shorten her cares and lengthen her days." [4]

*An apple pie without some cheese...*
*is like a kiss without a squeeze.*

# FRUIT

## BAKED APPLE DUMPLINGS (1700's)

Pastry crust, enough for two pies
8 medium or 6 large apples, peeled and cored
1/2 cup sugar mixed with 1 tsp. cinnamon and dash nutmeg
4 Tbs. butter

Roll crust out and cut into 6-8 inch squares. Place whole apple in middle of each square, sprinkle cinnamon-sugar mixture in hole along with a little butter. Bring pastry up to top of apple, press edges together and seal with a little water if needed. Chill for about an hour. Bake in a baking dish at 350° for about 15 minutes until they begin to brown, then add syrup.

> **Syrup:** Boil 2 cups water, one cup sugar, cinnamon, and a little butter for about 5 minutes. Add to apples and baste as they cook about 30 more minutes or until syrup has been mostly absorbed and apples are a nice brown.

**\*Note:** Choose your apple variety well for any cooked apple recipe. Golden Delicious and Winesap cook well and hold their shape. Don't use a Red Delicious to cook with. Eat them fresh.

## APPLE PIE

8 apples peeled, cored, and sliced thin
2 Tbs. flour
1/2 - 3/4 cup sugar depending on tartness of apples
1 tsp. cinnamon
Pinch of nutmeg and/or cloves

Stir apples, flour and spices together and pour into an uncooked pastry shell. Cover with a top crust that has a few slits cut in it for steam and juice to escape. To make a crumb crust, cut 1/4 cup butter with 1 cup flour and 1/3 cup brown sugar. Sprinkle on top of apples. Bake pie at 350° for up to an hour (until it bubbles). You may need to cover with foil at some point to prevent crust from burning before pie is cooked.

# FRUIT

## APPLE BUTTER

Cook quartered cooking apples in a small amount of water on low heat until tender. Cool slightly and strain through a food mill. To every 2 cups of pulp, add 1 cup of sugar. Add cinnamon sticks or powdered cinnamon to taste. Cook on stove on very low heat stirring with a wooden spoon constantly (or it will burn) for a *very long time*. You could get away with an hour or two of cooking, but real apple butter cooks stir it all day in a big iron pot outside on coals. Check to see if it is done by putting a spoonful on a plate; if no liquid forms around rim of sauce, it's done. Remove cinnamon sticks, refrigerate or seal in glass jars, and water process.

### Apple Wisdom
- *An apple never falls far from the tree.*
- *Reach for the high apples first; you can get the lower ones anytime.*
- *Apple pie order. Neat as apple pie. (Sayings originated from the sight of pies lined up orderly in a pie safe.)*

## OLD-FASHIONED APPLE STACK CAKE

| | |
|---|---|
| 1/2 cup buttermilk | 1 egg |
| 1/2 cup shortening | Flour |
| 1/2 tsp. soda | |
| 1/2 cup white sugar, 1/2 cup molasses (or all molasses) | |

Mix above ingredients well and add enough flour to make a stiff dough. Roll out into circles and bake on a greased cookie sheet until browned. Between cake layers, spread cooked dried apples flavored with cinnamon for a real intense flavor or use cooked fresh apples or any other fruit (cooked or fresh). Sprinkle top with powdered sugar.

# FRUIT

## FRUIT COBBLER

1 quart fruit (apple, peach, blueberry, blackberry, raspberry, cherry)
1 cup sugar, less if fruit very sweet, more if it's tart
3 Tbs. corn starch or flour, depending on juciness of fruit
raw sugar (turbinado) to sprinkle on top (optional)

Coat fruit with flour and sugar and put in bottom of a casserole pan or dutch oven.

*Top crust options:*
1. **One Pie Pastry**, sprinkled with raw sugar, cut slits for juice to escape and bake at 350° until bubbly.
2. **Sweetened Biscuit Dough.** Add 1/4 cup sugar to biscuit dough. You can either put a thin rolled dough on top of fruit, or cut out shapes and place on fruit. Sprinkle sugar on top. Bake at 350° until fruit bubbles and biscuits are done.
3. **Fruit Crisp.** Combine well by rubbing together with hands: 1 cup flour, 1/3 cup butter, 1/3 cup brown sugar, and a handful of oats. Nuts are good, too. Sprinkle on top of fruit and bake at 350° until bubbly.

**\*Note:** Your topping will try to get done before your fruit. If you make cobbler in a clear glass baking dish, you will know your fruit is cooked because the flour or corn starch will have turned from white to translucent. **Don't forget home-made vanilla ice cream!**

### Singing Superstitions:
•*If you sing before you eat,*
 *you will cry before you sleep.*
•*Singing before breakfast foretells*
 *anger before evening.*

# FRUIT

## SNAILS HOUSE COBBLER

Prepare fruit as in Fruit Cobbler recipe, and make a Sweet Biscuit dough. Roll the biscuit dough into a rectangular shape and sprinkle top with cinnamon sugar. Roll up jelly-roll fashion and slice off 1/2 inch sections, laying these on top of fruit. Bake at 350° until fruit bubbles and biscuits are browned.

*"Drying Apples by the Fireside", N.C. Archives and History*

## MIRACLE COBBLER

This is a fruit coffee cake that tastes great and is a snap to make.

| | |
|---|---|
| 2 Tbs. butter | 1 cup milk |
| 1 cup flour | 1 tsp. baking powder |
| 1 cup sugar | 1-2 cups berries, any kind |

Melt butter in an iron skillet. Stir dry ingredients together and add milk, mixing until no lumps remain. Pour into skillet with melted butter. Sprinkle berries over top and cook at 350° for about 35-40 minutes. Sugar sprinkled on top before baking adds a great touch.

> *Never work before breakfast. If you have to work*
> *before breakfast, eat your breakfast first.*
> -Josh Billings

# FRUIT

## FRESH FRUIT ROLY-POLY

2 eggs
1/2 cup milk
2 Tbs. melted butter

1/2 cup flour
3 Tbs. white sugar
Powdered sugar

Beat eggs, add milk, butter, flour, and white sugar. Pour into a large buttered iron skillet. Bake on lowest rack in oven for 20 min. at 450°. Reduce heat to 350° and cook about 15-20 min. longer. It will puff up. Remove to a platter and sprinkle with powdered sugar. Fill with fresh fruit when you're ready to serve.

## BLACKBERRY PIE

1 quart fresh blackberries
1 cup sugar
3 Tbs. flour, corn starch, or tapioca to thicken

Toss blackberries, sugar, and flour together and place in bottom of a unbaked pastry shell. Cover with a top crust, slit top to allow juice to escape, and bake at 350° for about an hour until berries bubble and crust is brown.

*Note: Blackberries have a mind of their own. You can't tell how juicy they are until you cook them. They actually make a better dish when cooked with a top crust only, because they can be too runny for a pie, especially wild varieties. If you have an abundant supply, experiment with different amounts of thickener to achieve the consistency you want.

*"A" is for apple, sour and green, working in Tommy but cannot be seen.*

# DESSERTS

Desserts were less common in pioneer times than now because "sweetnin'" was often scarce. Most folks kept a bee skep for honey, bought molasses from the general store when they could get there, and if times were real good, loaf sugar (white) could be had. Cakes were troublesome to bake, especially if there was no baking powder to raise it, so puddings were a popular dessert. Puddings were actually steamed cakes, and just about anything could be thrown in.

Shortening to make baked goods was another issue for settlers as butter was often rancid, imparting a bad taste to cookies and cakes, so that lard was more frequently used. The recipes in this section call for butter, but you can substitute margarine or solid vegetable shortening with good results. Lard makes a good pie crust, but is out of favor for cooking these days for health reasons.

## Cake Superstitions:

• Always stir the batter in one direction or you'll spoil the cake.
• It's bad luck to have more than one person stir the cake batter.
• If you should sneeze while baking a cake, say this rhyme out loud:

> *Sneeze on Monday, sneeze for fun,*
> *Sneeze on Tuesday, see someone,*
> *Sneeze on Wednesday, get a letter,*
> *Sneeze on Thursday, something better,*
> *Sneeze on Friday, sneeze for sorrow,*
> *Sneeze on Saturday, see your beau tomorrow,*
> *Sneeze on Sunday, the Devil will control you all week.*[9]

# DESToERTS

## DONUTS IN RHYME

One cup sugar, one cup milk
Two eggs beaten fine as silk

Salt and nutmeg (lemon will do)
Of baking powders teaspoons two

Gently stir the flour in
Roll on pie board not too thin

Cut in diamonds, twists or rings
Drop with care the doughy things

Into fat that swiftly swells
Evenly the spongy cells

Watch with care the fire for turning
Fry them brown, just short of burning

Roll in sugar, serve when cool
This a never failing rule.[5]

*by Mrs. Donald Stronsnider*

## 1883 Doughnut Alert:
*Do not eat doughnuts between April and November.[1]*

# DESSERTS

## CRUNCHY GINGERBREAD PEOPLE

1/2 cup butter
1/2 cup brown sugar
1/2 cup molasses
1 egg

1 tsp. baking soda
3 cups flour
1 tsp. powdered ginger
1-2 tsp. cinnamon

Cream butter, sugar, and molasses. Add egg. Mix dry ingredients and add to butter and sugar mixture. If the dough is too soft to roll out, chill for about an hour. Roll to desired thickness on a floured board, cut out, and decorate with raisins and nuts. Paint with a beaten egg white if you like the cookies shiny, and sprinkle with raw sugar. Bake at 350° about 10 minutes until they begin to brown. Remove at once from pan as they break easily.

## MRS. SMITH'S GINGERBREAD

2/3 cup shortening
1 cup brown sugar
1 cup molasses
2 eggs

3 cups flour
1 tsp. each soda & baking powder
1 tsp. each ginger & cinnamon
1 cup buttermilk

Cream shortening and sugar, add molasses and eggs. Stir together dry ingredients, and add alternately with buttermilk. Pour into a buttered and sugared oblong pan and bake at 350° for about 45 minutes or until cake springs back when touched.[12]

**Lemon Sauce Topping:** Serve on warm gingerbread.

Cook until thickened:
1 cup sugar
2 Tbs. corn starch
1 Tbs. butter

1 cup boiling water
1 lemon: juice & rind
Pinch of salt

| May our friendship spread like butter on hot gingerbread. |

# Desperts

## Sand Tarts (Jelly Tarts)

1 1/4 cup sugar
3/4 cup butter
1 egg, whole

1 egg white, slightly beaten
1 tsp. vanilla
3 cups flour (or a little less)

Beat sugar and butter until fluffy, add whole egg and vanilla. Gradually stir in flour until stiff dough is formed. Chill dough. Roll out thin on a pastry board, cut into circles. Brush each circle with egg white, then sprinkle with sugar and bake on greased cookie sheet at 350° until lightly browned....just a few minutes.

To make **Jelly Tarts**, put a teaspoonful of unchilled batter on a greased cookie sheet and press a hole in middle with your finger. Fill with jam when cooked or try putting a *little* raspberry or peach jam in the center before you bake.

## Fairy Cookies

2 cups sugar
1/2 cup butter
2 eggs
1 cup sour cream

1 tsp. soda
1 tsp. vanilla extract
Flour

Cream together sugar and butter. Add eggs, soda, sour cream, and extract. Add enough flour to make a soft dough. Roll out thin or drop spoonfuls onto greased cookie sheet. Bake at 350° until slightly browned.[7]

**Additions:** Dried fruit can be added to batter, sugar can be sprinkled on top, or a nut can be pressed in center of each cookie.

# DESSERTS

## MRS. PAINTER'S PUMPKIN PIE

3/4 cup brown sugar
1 Tbs. flour
1/2 tsp. salt
1 1/2 cup pumpkin (canned or fresh)
1 1/3 cup evaporated milk (can substitute whole milk)
1 slightly beaten egg
Spices:  1 tsp. cinnamon, 1/2 tsp. ginger and dash nutmeg

Mix ingredients well and pour into an unbaked pie crust.  Bake in a 350° oven for 30 minutes or until set.  Be careful not to burn crust.[12]

## Pastry Crust

**For one 9 inch pie:**
One cup flour                    1 tsp. sugar
1/3 cup shortening               Water, ice cold
1/2 tsp. salt

Cut shortening into dry ingredients and add water one tsp. at a time until dough barely sticks together.  Form into a ball and roll out into shape needed.  A tender, flaky crust depends on keeping dough chilled, using as little water as possible, and handling as little as possible.

> *Plant pumpkin seeds in May, and they will run away.*
> *Plant pumpkin seeds in June, and they will come too soon.*

# DESSERTS

## POOR MAN'S PUDDING, 1886

One egg, one cup sugar, one heaping Tbs. butter, one-half cup sweet milk, two cups flour, one tsp. baking powder. Beat egg, sugar, and butter together; add milk, then the flour and baking powder. Bake one-half hour; eat with sauce made of sugar and water, flavored to taste.[4]

## TOGUS BREAD

*A steamed pudding similar to Boston Brown Bread.*

Three cups of sweet milk, one cup of sour,
Three cups of Indian meal, one cup of flour,
Of soda sufficient a teaspoon to fill,
The same of salt and season it well,
A cup of molasses will make it quite sweet,
And a very good dish for a Yankee to eat.[9]
(Steam three hours).

**\*Note:** "Indian Meal" referred to cornmeal in pre-20th century cookbooks.

### Food Jump Rope Rhymes:

*Bake a pudding, bake a pie.*
*Did you ever tell a lie?*
*Yes, you did, you know you did.*
*You broke your mama's teapot lid.*

*Apple, peaches, pumpkin pie.*
*How many years before I die?*
*1-2-3......*

# FAUX FOODS

About the only faux food people hear of today is "Mock Apple Pie," made of crackers. While the idea is intriguing, we don't need to make it because apples are readily available. Pioneer resourcefulness took over where scarcity left off, yielding many creative food substitutes so that families didn't have to do without their favorite dishes. In fact, if you look at cook books dating up until the 1950's, you'll find plenty of mock recipes and many of them are quite tasty. The recipes that follow date from 1833 through 1954.

## MOCK CLAM CHOWDER

Prepare clam chowder but leave out the clams, add a little more salt and cook a little longer.

## MOCK OLIVES

Soak full grown green grapes 48 hrs. in salt and water, then scald with strong vinegar.

## MOCK OYSTERS

2 cups grated corn (corn kernals)
1 egg
Cracker meal, enough to bind together
Salt and pepper to taste

Combine ingredients and saute in a buttered skillet until brown and cooked through. (Known to us today as corn fritters).

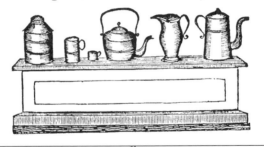

# Faux Foods

## Mock Mince Pie (1886)

Pioneer mince pie was a handy way to use scraps of meats and even vegetables. Dried fruit and molasses were added for sweetness. The recipe that follows bears more resemblance to the mince pie we're familiar with today.

"Two eggs, two crackers, one-half cup vinegar, one teaspoon all kinds of spice, one cup sugar, one cup molasses, one cup hot water, currants, and raisins. Pour in uncooked pie shell and bake until done."[4]

## Mock Pecan Pie (Oatmeal Pie)

*Here's a modern version of a tasty, economical mock pecan pie. This is REALLY good.*

2 eggs
1/2 cup white sugar
3/4 cup old fashion oats (not quick cooking)
3/4 cup dark corn syrup
3/4 cup coconut
2 Tbs. melted butter

Combine ingredients and pour into an unbaked pie shell. Bake at 350° until it looks done. The oats will be on the top. The pie will be brown and bubbly.

> *If you would have a hen lay, you must bear with her cackling.*
> *-Thomas Fuller*

# FAUX FOODS

## MOCK WHIPPED CREAM FILLING

1 1/2 cup grated apple, peach, or mashed berries
1 1/2 cups sugar
white of 2 eggs
grated rind of 1 lemon

Mix all together and beat until very stiff. Use between and on top of layer cakes or as a cake filling. (Eating raw eggs is not recommended. Use imitation whipped topping for substitute).

## MOCK ANGEL FOOD CAKE

1 cup sugar
11/2 cup pastry flour
3 tsp. baking powder
1/4 cup softened butter
pinch salt

1/2 cup cold water
1 tsp. vanilla
2 egg whites

Mix together dry and wet ingredients separately, then add wet to dry and beat hard until smooth. Pour batter into a small ungreased angel food cake pan and cook in a slow oven. When cake rises to top of the pan, turn heat up to about 350° and bake until firm.

*William A. Barnhill Collection, Pack Mem. Library, Asheville, NC*

> *The cook was a good cook, as cooks go;*
> *and as cooks go, she went.*
> -H.H. Munro

# BEVERAGES

W ell water was often contaminated by farm animals and outhouses, so early settlers fared best when it was boiled before drinking. Thus, hot beverages, fruit drinks, and fermented drinks were the norm. Coffee was one of the most sought-after staples that had to be purchased at the general store. Beans were bought green and roasted at home. Every homestead owned a hand turned coffee mill and beans were carefully ground only as needed. Boiled coffee was most common with egg shells added to settle the grounds. Some cooks tied the grounds up in muslin bags to be dunked in boiling water. Coffee substitutes included chicory, parched peas, beans, or potatoes.

Tea came and went in popularity in the 1800's, and could be found at times in the general store, but was often made from herbs locally cultivated or gathered and given to the sick. Fermented drinks made their way to the tables of most households and even beer was called a good family beverage in the early 1800's!

## PIONEER BEVERAGES:

Home-brewed beer
Wine
Cordials made from fruit
Apple and pear cider
Honey and water

Milk and buttermilk
Grape juice
Tea
Sassafrass tea and herb tea
Coffee

*"Make my coffee strong enough to float an egg!"*

---

### A Toast to the Farmer in 1810

*Farmer at the plough,*
*Wife milking cow,*
*Daughter spinning yarn,*
*Son threshing in the barn,*
*All happy to a charm.*

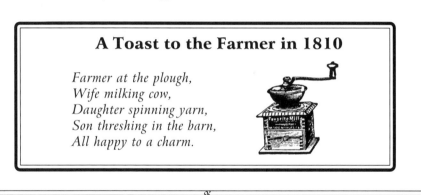

# BEVERAGES

## CHERRY BOUNCE

Take 1/2 gallon wild (or tame) cherries, and put in a 5 gallon crock. Add the same amount of water and one pound sugar. Mash well. Add 1 qt. brandy and let it set for about 4 months, mashing and stirring with a wooden spoon from time to time. Strain seeds and pulp, and pour liquid into jars, seal, and let rest for another month, then sip slowly![7]

## BLACKBERRY WINE

Put 2 gallons fresh picked blackberries in a crock and cover with water. Mash and stir well several times during the day. By nightfall, strain into a large container and add 3 1/2 cups sugar to each gallon of juice. Dissolve 1/2 pkg. yeast in 1/4 cup water and add to juice/sugar mix and stir well. Ferment until it stops working, and then put in jugs and cover tops with cloth. Let continue to work in a warm place until bubbles cease to rise. When completely fermented, seal, and drink the following spring.[7]

## GINGER BEER (NON-ALCOHOLIC)

Fresh ginger root the size of your thumb
1 lemon, squeezed
1 cup sugar
1 tsp. dry yeast
1 tsp. cream of tartar

Smash the ginger root (one good whack with a rolling pin) and add it to 2 quarts boiling water along with the lemon juice and the sugar. When mixture cools to lukewarm, add yeast and cream of tartar. Stir until yeast dissolves. Cover and let stand overnight. In the morning, pour liquid into clean bottles and cork for old-timey effect. Leave sediment in pan. Let bottles stand at room temperature for 3-4 days until fermented. Chill, then enjoy.

*Warning: If left to ferment too long, beverage will blow cork out. Check after 2 days to see if it's bubbly, chill as soon as it reaches this stage.

# BUTTER

M uch was written about good and bad butter in 19th century cookbooks. Lack of adequate refrigeration and milk's affinity for absorbing nearby odors made fresh tasting butter a rare find. As Betty Botter can attest to, buying it from the store didn't guarantee a good product either!

## Betty Botter

*Betty Botter bought some butter. "But," she said, "this butter's bitter.*
*If I put this bitter butter in my batter, it would make my batter bitter.*
*But a bit of better butter would but make my bitter batter better."*
*So Betty Botter bought some butter, better than the bitter butter.*
*Made her bitter batter better.*

Butter was (and still is) made by skimming the cream from milk. The cream was collected for a few days until there was enough to churn. Most churns were tall and wooden with a hole in the middle

*Edward M. Ball ollection, Pack Memorial Library, Asheville, N.C.*

for the dasher. The dasher was a long pole with crossed wood at the bottom that was moved up and down to agitate the cream. When the butter formed (came), it was scooped out of the buttermilk and put in a bowl of cold water to be washed over and over until every drop of milk was gone. Salting, kneading, then molding finished off the task. Butter churning was time consuming and tedious and all kinds of butter churning charms, jingles, and songs were created to make the job more fun.

# BUTTER

## HOME-MADE BUTTER

Put some room-temperature whipping cream in a jar with a tight fitting lid. Shake hard for a long time until butter flakes are visible. Continue shaking until mixture thickens. Wash the butter by compacting the flakes together and running very cold water over until no more milk can be rinsed out. Salt it, or leave it "sweet".

You can mold it by pressing into butter molds if you have them, or press into candy molds, chill, then pop them out and place in an air-tight container.

N.C. Archives and History

---

### Dairy Wisdom

• *He who has butter on his bread should not stand in the sun.*
*-Yiddish Proverb*
• *The world is your cow, but you have to do the milking.*

---

# Honey & Molasses

Sweetnin' for early pioneer cooking was more likely found than bought. Settlers robbed honey from wild hives or lured bees to their own bee "gums". If a family lived near a general store and had money, they could buy white or brown sugar in compressed loaves. Molasses was much less expensive, and more available, therefore most recipes were adapted to accomodate it. In the northern climates, maple syrup was made at "sugarin'-off" parties, where the sap was (and still is) boiled down at a ratio of 40:1 in kettles over a slow fire.

## Molasses Taffy

Combine one cup molasses, one of sugar, one Tbs. vinegar or lemon juice, and a piece of butter the size of a walnut. Boil twenty-five minutes, stirring constantly until it reaches the hard ball stage. (A bit dropped into cold water forms a hard ball). Pour it out onto a greased plate without stirring first. When cool enough to handle, pull taffy with buttered hands, then snip into bite-size pieces. If you make this with children, have them keep their distance until taffy is ready to pull. (You start to pull then hand it to them to finish).

**The fine art of taffy pulling:** Grab a partner and a chunk of warm taffy. Each of you will take an end and pull the candy out, folding it back on itself. The candy will whiten as air becomes trapped in it and it will become stiff, but stop before it's grainy.

### Old-Time Speedometer

• *Slow as molasses, warm as toast.*
• *Slow as molasses in January running up a hill.*

# BEESWAX

P ioneers preferred candles made from beeswax as they smelled good and burned slowly. Beeswax was quite a luxury so that most candles were made from beef or sheep tallow. They smelled of burning fat as they were used, but were effective.

## DIP YOUR OWN CANDLES

Buy some beeswax (or parafin) at a craft store. Place small pieces in a tin can which is then placed in a crock pot in a few inches of water. Put the lid on the crockpot and cook on low heat until wax is melted (about one hour). Please keep away from children. Cut some candlewicking the length of two candles. Hold wick in middle and dip both ends in wax quickly. If the wax does not hold well to the wick, try letting your wax cool a little. Repeat dipping over and over until desired thickness is achieved. Hang to dry.

**\*Note:** If you are doing this activity with children (no younger than eight), they can dip their wick in very cold water between wax dips to speed up the process. Supervise well!

*"Bee Gums", N.C. Archives and History*

*"Bee Gums"*

### Sweet Advice

• *You can catch more flies with honey than you can with vinegar.*
• *For sweetness honey, for love, a wife.*
• *If bees stay at home, rain will soon come; If they fly away, fine will be the day.*

# 1800's Remedies

Remedies were found at the back of all nineteenth century cookbooks. Folk medicine was the norm, and many remedies were made from food items. Some were effective, some probably toxic. The remedies that follow are from old cookbooks and are not recommended for actual use unless you run out of toothpaste and don't mind using chalk and soap as a substitute!

### Receipt For A Long Life

*Nor love, nor honor, wealth, nor power,*
*Can give the heart a cheerful hour,*
*When health is lost. Be timely wise;*
*With health all taste of pleasure lies.*
*-Gay*
*The ingredients of health and long life are*
*Great temperance, open air,*
*Easy labor, little care.*
*-sir Philip Sidney*

## For Bilious Affections and Dropsy

Steep one oz. dandelion in a jug with a pint of boiling water for fifteen minutes. Sweeten with brown sugar or honey, and drink several cupfuls during the day. (1852)

# 1800's Remedies

### To Prevent Lamp Smoking
Soak the wick in strong vinegar and dry it well before using.

### Bed Bug Poison
Scotch snuff mixed with soft soap.

### Cure for Tape Worms
Chew pumpkin seeds before bed.

### Frosted Feet
Dip feet in water, dry with a coarse towel. Put immediately into a pail of brine brought from a pickle tub.[6]

### Musquito (sic) Bites
Salt wetted into a paste, with a little vinegar and rubbed on bite will stop the itch.[6]

### To Stop Blood
For a prick with a pin, or a slight cut, nothing stops bleeding better than old cobwebs compressed into a lump and applied to a wound.[6]

### Diarrhea
Blackberry wine. Blackberry tea. Blackberries.

### In Case You're Struck by Lightening
"For a couple of hours shower in cold water. In case there is still no sign of life, add a cupful of salt and continue for another hour."[7]
-19th century Swiss remedy

### Wrinkle Remover
Combine two oz. of honey, two oz. juice of the lilly bulb, and one oz. of melted wax. Apply to the face night and morning.

### Uses for Ear Wax
Prevents pain from injury by nail or skewer. "Those who are troubled by cracked lips have found this remedy successful when others have failed. It is one of those sorts of cures, which are very likely to be laughed at; but I know of its having produced very beneficial results." (1833)[2]

# 1800's Remedies

## Corns
Bind on thick slices of lemon.[4]

## Tooth Powder (Toothpaste)
Take pulverized chalk, and twice as much charcoal; make very fine, and add castile soap suds and spirits of camphor to make a thick paste. Apply with the finger and brush.[4]

## To Prevent the Hair Coming Out
Bathe the head in salt water. This will also make the hair thicker.[4]

## Plaster
There is no better plaster for wounds or cuts, than the inside lining of a freshly broken eggshell, if applied immediately.[4]

## Drawn Sinews
An ointment made from the common ground-worms which boys dig to bait fishes, rubbed on with the hand, is said to be excellent when the sinews are drawn up by any disease or accident.[2]

## General Maxims for Health
Rise early, eat simple food, take plenty of exercise. Let not children be dressed in tight clothes. Avoid the necessity of a physician, but if you find yourself really ill, have nothing to do with quacks or quack medicine. Keep hair clean, washing does not injure the hair as is generally supposed. Do not sleep with hair braided or frizzled. Do not make children cross-eyed, by having hair hang about their foreheads, where they see it continually. (1833)

---

•*He who sows hurry, reaps indigestion.*
                    *-Robert Louis Stevenson*
•*Eat an apple going to bed, knock the doctor on the head.*

# REMEDIES

## GRUEL

You've probably been searching all your life for a good gruel recipe to feed your sick loved-ones. Here's one from 1833:

"Gruel is very easily made. Have a pint of water boiling in the skillet; stir up three or four large spoonfuls of nicely sifted oatmeal, rye, or Indian (cornmeal), in cold water. Pour it into the skillet while the water boils. Let it boil eight or ten minutes. Throw in a large handful of raisins to boil, if the patient is well enough to bear them. When put in a bowl, add a little salt, white sugar, and nutmeg."[2]

*Photo by Margaret Morley, N.C. Archives*

*"A Mountain Home"*

R.H. Scadin Collection, Ramsey Library, UNCA, Asheville, N.C.

## When Mandy Starts to Wash

When Mandy sets the water on,
And hustles up the fire,
And starts a stirrin' up the starch
And hiests her sleeves up higher,
Why, then you know the war is on,
It ain't no time to josh,
The only thing to do is ...git!
When Mandy starts to wash.

Cold beans and bread and coffee's all
I'll get to eat that day.
And ain't no use to stay around
And git in Mandy's way.
For then, she'll set me hard at work
A-rinsin out...kersplosh
You can't stay round the house and shirk
When Mandy starts to wash![5]

*-Author Unknown*

# GRAIN AND SEED SOURCES

## STONE GROUND CORNMEAL AND FLOUR

Brewster River Mill
Mill Street
Jeffersonville, VT 05464
(802)644-2987

Burnt Cabins Grist Mill
Burnt Cabins, PA 17215
(717)987-3244

Butte Creek Mill
PO Box 561
Eagle Point, OR 97524
(503)826-3531

Falls Mill & Country Store
Rt. 1, PO Box 44
Belvedere, TN 37306
(615)469-7161

Gray's Grist Mill
PO Box 422
Adamsville, RI  02801
(508)636-6075

Ledgord Mill & Museum
RR#2,  PO Box 152
Wartrace, TN 37183
(615)455-1935

Morgan's Mills
RD #2, PO Box 115
Union, ME 04862
(207)785-4900

Old Mill of Guilford
1340 NC 68 North
Oak Ridge, NC 27310
(919)643-4783

## HEIRLOOM SEEDS

Bountiful Gardens
19550 Walker Road
Willilts, CA 95490

Johnny's Selected Seeds
299 Foss Hill Road
Albion, ME 04910

Seed Savers Exchange
R.R. 3, Box 239
Decorah, IA 52101

Shepherd's Garden Seeds
30 Irene Street
Torrington, CT 06790

The Cook's Garden
P.O. Box 65
Londonderry, VT 05148

# CREDITS

1. Buckeye Pub. Co., *The Buckeye Cookbook*, 1883. Reprint. Dover Publications, N.Y., 1975. 2. Child, Mrs., *The American Frugal Housewife*, 1833. Reprint. Applewood Books, MA.. 3. Culinary Arts Press, *Pennsylvania Dutch Cookbook*, 1960. 4. Cushing, Mrs. C. H. and Gray, Mrs. B., *The Kansas Home Cook Book*, 1886. Reprint. Arno Press, New York, 1973. 5. Harrison Co. Ext. Homemakers, *W.Va. Heritage Cookbook*, 1976. 6. Leslie, Eliza, *Directions for Cookery, in its Various Branches*, 1848. Reprint. Arno Press, New York, 1973. 7. Mailloux, Eleanor, *Oppis Guit's Vo Helvetia*. Helvetia, W.Va. 8. Marcy, Randolph, The Prairie Traveler, 1859. Reprint. Applewood Books, MA. 9. Reed, Ethel, *Pioneer Kitchen, A Frontier Cookbook*. Frontier Heritage Press, Los Angeles, Ca., 1971. 10. Rosser, Linda, *Pioneer Cooking Around Oklahoma*. Bobwhite Publications, OK., 1978. 11. Schlissel, Lillian. *Women's Diaries of the Westward Journey*, Schocken Books, N.Y., 1982. 12. United Methodist Women, *The Art of Cooking in Salem*. Salem, W. Va. 13. Walker, Barbara, *The Little House Cookbook*. Scholastic, Inc., New York, 1979. 14. Webster, Mrs. A.L, *The Improved Housewife, or Book of Receipts by a Married Lady*. 1845. Reprint. Arno Press, New York, 1973. 15. The Great Smokey Mountains Natural History Assoc., *Mountain Makin in the Smokies, a Cookbook*. 1957. Title page photo: *Edward M. Ball Collection, Asheville, NC*. Back cover photo of Barbara Swell by *Wayne Erbsen*.

# THANKS!

Thanks to the women in my life who loved to cook and didn't shoo me out of their kitchens when I was a kid: Nancy Swell, Maudie Smith, Mary Ellen Smith (my mom, grandmother, and aunt). Food victims...I mean critics included Annie, Rita, and Wes Erbsen, Wayne Erbsen, Tracy McMahon, and Joe Bruno. They're still alive to date. Thanks to Janet Swell for editing, Steve Millard for cover design and all around art directorship, Jean Harrison, Richard Renfro, Marti Otto, Johnny Otto (my biscuit hero), Loretta and John Erbsen for sharing old and new cookbooks. Appreciation as well to Leon Swell for computer support, Laura Wright for reminiscing about our family of cooks, Adrian Holifield for Betty Botter, and Doug Elliot for Zucchini Claranet.

# RECIPE INDEX